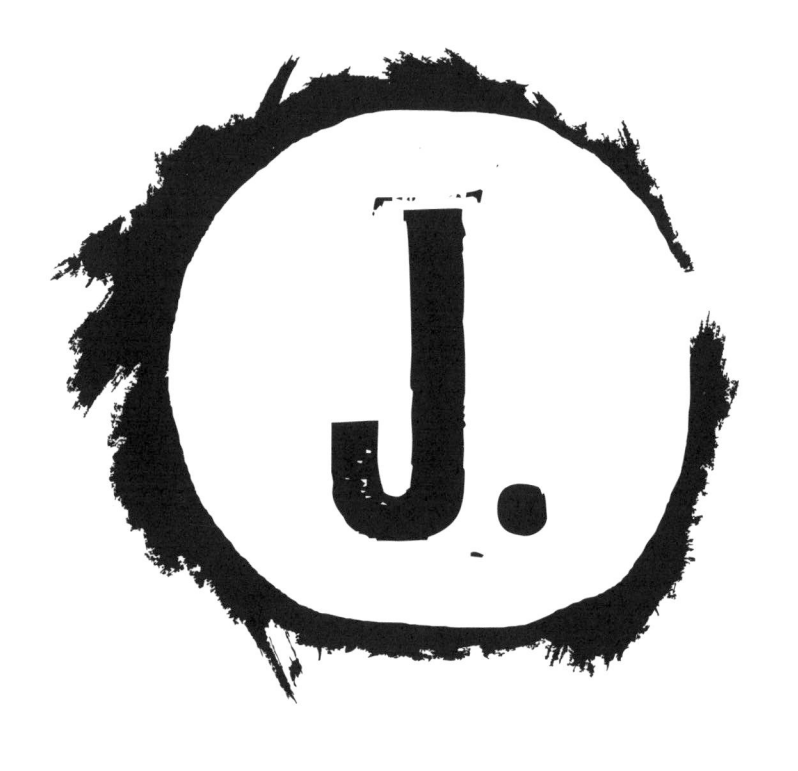

JESUS-CENTERED
SMALL GROUP BIBLE STUDIES

7 Sessions for Discovering Jesus
in the Old and New Testaments

Loveland, CO

Group
Real. **Bold**. Love.

Group resources really work!

This Group resource incorporates our R.E.A.L. approach to ministry. It reinforces a growing friendship with Jesus, encourages long-term learning, and results in life transformation, because it's:

Relational—Learner-to-learner interaction enhances learning and builds Christian friendships.

Experiential—What learners experience through discussion and action sticks with them up to 9 times longer than what they simply hear or read.

Applicable—The aim of Christian education is to equip learners to be both hearers and doers of God's Word.

Learner-based—Learners understand and retain more when the learning process takes into consideration how they learn best.

JESUS-CENTERED SMALL GROUP BIBLE STUDIES

7 Sessions for Discovering Jesus in the Old and New Testaments
LEADER GUIDE

Copyright © 2016 Group Publishing, Inc. / 0000 0001 0362 4853

Visit our website: **group.com**

Credits

Session Writers: Rick Edwards and Mikal Keefer

Senior Editor: Mikal Keefer

Managing Editor: Craig Cable

Editor: Rick Edwards

Assistant Editor: Ann Diaz

Art and Design: Darrin Stoll

ISBN 978-1-4707-4276-8 (Paperback)
ISBN 978-1-4707-4280-5 (ePub)

Printed in the United States of America.

10 9 8 7 6 5 4 3 2   25 24 23 22 21 20 19 18 17 16

JESUS-CENTERED
SMALL GROUP BIBLE STUDIES

INTRODUCTION

We're delighted that you want to grow closer to Jesus and experience the unique features of your *Jesus-Centered Bible* by using these seven 1-hour studies.

Your Bible uses blue letters to identify references to Jesus in the Old Testament, so you'll easily discover how Jesus has been present and active throughout all of history. You'll encounter Jesus in every session, again and again, in fresh ways.

Use these studies in a small group, a Sunday school class, or anywhere you gather with friends who want to know Jesus better.

These studies are engaging, active, and ready for your use—so dive in!

TIPS FOR LEADING JESUS-CENTERED BIBLE STUDIES

Each session aims to have you do two things: (1) discover some aspect(s) of Jesus' identity as revealed or foreshadowed in the Old Testament sources, and (2) explore and reflect on your identity in Christ. "The closer we get to Jesus, the more we discover our true identity and purpose in life" (*Jesus-Centered Bible*, page A6).

Because Jesus wants to be in relationship with us, these Bible studies are highly relational. Much of the time, participants will meet in small groups of two or four people. These groups serve as natural incubators for personal sharing and expression, self-discovery, and relationship building—all while maximizing participation.

These Bible studies are also fun and interactive, so people fully engage with each other and with the Bible. This ensures that your study group members will not only learn and retain information about Jesus, but they will also know and experience Jesus on a personal level that results in lasting transformation.

Living out our Jesus-shaped identity can be done only through our real-life thoughts and actions. So we've included some practical ways of staying connected to Jesus after each session is complete. Make copies of the **Abiding in Jesus** activities at the end of each session's instructions. Encourage participants to try the ideas on these take-home pages, and ask follow-up questions when you gather again.

USING YOUR JESUS-CENTERED BIBLE

Here are short descriptions of the unique features of the *Jesus-Centered Bible* that you'll be using while leading these Bible studies. Your time together will be more fun and productive if you take a few minutes up front to familiarize yourself and your study group with these features. (You can find even more details and tips on pages A6-A13 of the *Jesus-Centered Bible* itself.)

BLUE-LETTER TEXT

The *Jesus-Centered Bible* uses blue-letter print to highlight Old Testament passages that refer to Jesus, such as prophecies, themes, and verses that Jesus quoted.

BLUE EXPLANATION BOXES

Accompanying each blue-letter passage in the Old Testament is a blue box at the bottom of the page. These boxes make explicit the connections between the passage and Jesus, including links to relevant New Testament passages.

"JESUS IN EVERY BOOK" ESSAYS

Each book of the *Jesus-Centered Bible* features an introduction that gives a surprising, profound, and personal perspective on Jesus' story in that book—a story that weaves like a golden thread through the tapestry of the entire Bible.

"REFRAMING JESUS" SIDEBARS

Scattered throughout the Old and New Testaments, these short pieces offer interesting context, surprising backstories, and penetrating theological insights that highlight the beauty of Jesus in that particular section of Scripture.

JESUS QUESTIONS

Just as Jesus used surprising and personal questions to prompt deeper reflection, the *Jesus-Centered Bible* scatters throughout the New Testament more than 100 questions about Jesus and our relationship with him.

RED-LETTER NAMES OF JESUS

The words of Jesus spoken in the four New Testament gospels are printed in red, just as in many other Bibles. However, the *Jesus-Centered Bible* goes a step further by printing in red *any* name, nickname, or title that clearly refers to Jesus in the New Testament writings.

LIFE'S ESSENTIAL QUESTIONS

Nine of life's biggest, most significant questions are raised several times in the New Testament gospels. The *Jesus-Centered Bible* highlights those questions, as well as Jesus' penetrating responses to them.

To lead these studies, you need only this leader guide and the *Jesus-Centered Bible,* along with a few simple supplies. Each participant will also need a copy of the *Jesus-Centered Bible.* Journals are available and make a great optional companion piece for participants who want to dig deeper throughout the week.

- *Jesus-Centered Bible*, available in hardcover and imitation leather

- *Jesus-Centered Journal,* available in turquoise, charcoal, saddle, and cranberry

May we also suggest…

- *The Jesus-Centered Life* by Rick Lawrence

These resources can be purchased at group.com or from your favorite Christian retailer.

SESSION 1:
CREATOR JESUS

SESSION SUMMARY

In this session you'll encounter Jesus as Creator and discover you're among his loved and valued creations. Not only are you created in his image, but you've been given the opportunity to help care for some of his creation.

ⓙ SUPPLIES NEEDED:

- A copy of the *Jesus-Centered Bible* for each person

- Blank sheet of paper and a pencil for each person

- A photocopy of the "Abiding in Jesus" take-home page for each person

---

1. GATHERING

(60 MINUTES REMAIN; USE 8 MINUTES IN THIS SECTION)

Greet participants and welcome them warmly. Give everyone a blank sheet of paper and a pencil.

Say: **Picture for a moment a favorite place in nature. Perhaps you love walking along an ocean beach or hiking in the mountains. Or maybe you're fascinated by watching the tigers at the zoo or snorkeling with colorful fish along a coral reef. Take a few minutes to draw a quick sketch of a favorite spot in nature.**

Don't worry if your drawing doesn't fully capture the beauty of the spot you have in mind; you'll get a chance to describe it.

After several minutes, ask participants to form small groups of four persons each.

> Say: **It's time for show and tell! Show the others in your small group what you drew and tell them what makes that spot in nature special to you.**
>
> Allow several minutes for conversation; give a one-minute warning to wrap up conversation by saying: **Take another minute to talk in your small group.**
>
> When a minute has passed, say: **Thanks for sharing your sketches and your stories. Hang onto your sketch and pencil; you'll need them again.**
>
> **You know, lots of people find a spiritual connection with God through nature. Here's something else for you to talk about in your group of four:**
>
> ❷ **What, if anything, does your special spot in nature tell you about God?**

Allow several minutes for small groups to talk, and then give a one-minute warning to wrap up conversation.

2. NOTICING JESUS

(52 MINUTES REMAIN; USE 10 MINUTES IN THIS SECTION)

Ask participants to turn to Genesis 1:1-2 (p. 5) in their copies of the *Jesus-Centered Bible* and follow along as a volunteer reads aloud both Genesis 1:1-2 and the Blue Explanation Box at the bottom of page 5. (All page numbers refer to the *Jesus-Centered Bible.*)

Then ask for a volunteer to read aloud John 1:1-5 (p. 1107).

Say: **Christians often focus on Jesus as Savior...but he's more. He's also Creator.**

Creator of that spot in nature you talked about and Creator of the cosmos. And, more to the point, Creator of us—of you and me.

If we're going to notice Jesus for who he is, in the Bible and in life, we have to notice him as Creator.

A question for you in your small group:

❓ **How well did Jesus do as Creator, would you say? If you were giving Creator Jesus a grade for the work he did—in the universe and in you—what grade would you give him, and why?**

Allow several minutes for small groups to talk, and then give a one-minute warning to wrap up conversation.

Ask: **Where did you land with grades? Anyone willing to share with the whole group what you discussed in your small group of four?**

Allow time for reporting back from the smaller groups.

3. CREATOR JESUS

(42 MINUTES REMAIN, USE 5 MINUTES IN THIS SECTION)

Say: **Thanks for sharing your insights.**

Maybe you haven't thought much about Jesus as Creator.

Many Christians have Jesus in a box that opens on Christmas morning in Bethlehem and closes as Jesus rises back to heaven after his resurrection. They know they'll

see him again at the great Resurrection when he returns, but they haven't thought much about what he did before the manger and what he's up to now...

Which includes, according to the Bible, creating. Jesus is identified as Creator in both the Old and New Testaments—as demonstrated in the passages we just read.

A question for us as a whole group:

❓ **In what way, if any, does your image of Jesus change when you think of him as creator of the universe?**

Allow time for whole group discussion.

4. JESUS IN JOHN

(37 MINUTES REMAIN, USE 8 MINUTES IN THIS SECTION)

Ask participants to turn to page 1106 of their *Jesus-Centered Bibles* and to follow along as a volunteer reads aloud the "Jesus in John" essay.

After the volunteer finishes, read aloud again the fourth paragraph—the one beginning with "Matthew begins with a genealogy from Abraham..."

Say: **We sometimes picture a creator as a solitary sculptor working in a studio, or a painter sitting alone trying to capture a landscape on canvas.**

That's not how Jesus creates. According to the Bible, Jesus is part of a relationship—Father, Son, and Holy Spirit—and he's a co-creator of all we see and experience.

Jesus is all about relationships—with God, the Holy Spirit, and with us. He's still shaping us as we grow, and stands ready to collaborate with us as we express our God-given creativity.

Our creativity might be expressed in the arts...or the kitchen...in parenting...or as we reach a solution to a problem at work. Jesus' work in and through us isn't yet done.

Ask participants to huddle up with their groups of four again and to discuss this:

❷ **Tell about a time you've experienced Jesus creating something in or through you. What happened—and how did it feel?**

5. ANIMAL IMPROVEMENTS

(29 MINUTES REMAIN; USE 10 MINUTES IN THIS SECTION)

Thank participants for sharing their stories, and then ask them to turn over their papers so they can draw on the back side.

Ask everyone to draw an animal improvement they'd consider making.

For instance, they might draw a dog who can drive—so road trips with the family Fido are easier. Or a cat with opposable thumbs—so it can open its own food tins. Or a kangaroo big enough to carry them in its pouch.

Tell participants they can improve on any animal they want, and they can make as many improvements as they wish... but they have just three minutes to sketch.

After three minutes have passed, invite participants to share with their small groups what they drew—and why. Allow up to two minutes for this.

6. PRAYER

(19 MINUTES REMAIN; USE 4 MINUTES IN THIS SECTION)

Say: **Jesus is a Creator—and he has the power to improve on his designs in nature (though he might not necessarily sign off on our suggestions!).**

But he very much wants to hear your ideas about making changes for a particular spot in nature...and he's very willing to engage with you in making them. That spot is your own life.

Let's pause for a moment to tell Jesus where we could use his help making changes in our lives.

Perhaps it's letting go of a past hurt. Or you need help with a physical condition. Maybe you know you're not faithfully following him in some area of your life.

Whatever it is, silently tell Jesus about it as we sit quietly for several minutes. Be honest and open—this is your chance to invite the Creator of the universe into your life in a fresh way to continue in you the good work he's started.

I'll close our time of prayer after two minutes of silence.

After two minutes, say: **Thank you for your love and power, Jesus. Thank you for hearing us. Amen.**

7. HOW'S IT FEEL?

(15 MINUTES REMAIN; USE 4 MINUTES IN THIS SECTION)

Say: **Thank you. I won't ask you to share what you and Jesus talked about; that's between the two of you.**

But in your small group, please talk about this:

❓ **How much hope do you have that Jesus will somehow help you deal with what you discussed? Why do you answer as you do?**

8. REFLECTING JESUS

(11 MINUTES REMAIN; USE 8 MINUTES IN THIS SECTION)

Say: **Creator Jesus has given us an opportunity to help manage what he's created. Let's pause to consider how well we're handling the honor.**

Ask a volunteer to read aloud Genesis 1:26-31 (p. 6). Then ask the whole group this question:

❓ **Overall, how's humanity doing taking care of this planet? Why do you answer as you do?**

After several responses, ask each person to find a partner and discuss this question:

❓ **Forget humanity. How are *you* doing caring for *your* corner of the planet? What's something you're doing well, and what's something you'd consider changing so you could do an even better job?**

After three minutes, ask for volunteers to share with the larger group what they discussed with their partners. After several people have shared, move to section 9.

9. CROWNED WITH GLORY

(3 MINUTES REMAIN; USE 3 MINUTES IN THIS SECTION)

Thanks for considering how you're reflecting Creator Jesus—and how you can stay connected to him both *as his creation* and as someone serving him in *managing his creation*.

By the way, you're quite the creation! Let's celebrate that by grabbing our *Jesus-Centered Bibles* and reading together Psalm 8 (p. 564).

Ask participants to take turns reading verses until you've finished all nine verses of the psalm.

ABIDING IN JESUS

Want to interact more with Creator Jesus? Try this activity.

Spend 30 minutes outdoors in some natural setting: park, garden, forest, wildlife preserve. Use the first 15 minutes for silent observation, simply writing notes just as a naturalist would: describe plants, wildlife, sights and sounds, and so on.

Next, take another 15 minutes to read two passages from the *Jesus-Centered Bible:* Colossians 1:15-17 (pp. 1241-1242) and Hebrews 1:1-3 (p. 1277) and then reflect on these four questions, either in silent reflection or by writing down your thoughts and impressions:

❓ What meaning do these verses give to the observations of nature you just wrote?

_____

_____

❓ In these Scriptures, what is the relationship between creation, Jesus, and God?

_____

_____

❓ What do these passages say to you about God's heart for people and creation?

_____

_____

❓ How will your reflections affect *your* relationship with God, with others, and with creation?

_____

_____

SESSION 2:
JESUS, THE SECOND—AND BETTER!—ADAM

SESSION SUMMARY

In this session you'll explore the damaging effects of sin in the world by reading the story of Adam and Eve. You'll also discover how anyone can be rescued from a life controlled by sin because of what Jesus, the "Second Adam," did to reverse the damage done by the first Adam.

(J.) SUPPLIES NEEDED:

- A copy of the *Jesus-Centered Bible* for each person
- A wallet-sized photo or cell phone photo of one of your loved ones
- A photocopy of the "Abiding in Jesus" take-home page for each person

---

1. GATHERING

(60 MINUTES REMAIN; USE 8 MINUTES IN THIS SECTION)

Greet participants and welcome them warmly.

Begin this session by asking everyone to form groups of four people each. Then ask them to search their purses, wallets, or cell phones for a photo of a spouse, child, or another loved one. A photo of a pet or a highly prized possession such as a car or a garden would also work.

If someone doesn't have a photo available, he or she can select an object that represents a loved one. For example, a jointly held credit card, a note, a pacifier, a sock, a candy wrapper, or another object can stand in for a photo.

Say: **In a few moments, I'm going to ask you to show your small group of four the photo or object you've selected and to tell about the person or possession it represents. Tell those nice people you're with why what you're showing is precious to you.**

To model what participants are to do next, including the vulnerability you hope to see, briefly display the photo you've brought of a loved one. Tell why you care about the person and any memory you have of the place or time the photo was taken.

Say: **That's my show-and-tell photo. Now, in your group of four, display yours. Tell what or who is in the photo and why you care so deeply about the person or object. And if there's a story about where or when the photo was shot, tell that, too.**

Allow up to four minutes. When groups have about a minute left to share, say: **Take another minute; then I'll be calling your attention back to me.**

After 60 seconds, call for the attention of participants and continue.

Say: **Our photos or objects prompted some great conversation—and pausing to look at them evoked some emotions, didn't it? Which is pretty amazing considering that the photos and objects aren't actually what we care about.**

They're just representations. I may have a great photo of my friend, but that's not the same thing as having my friend in the room.

Today we're going to get to know Jesus in a way that might seem a bit...odd. We're going to get to know Jesus by looking at someone who represents him.

We'll meet someone who's *not* Jesus, but who's been held up as a *representation* of Jesus.

Let's dive in.

2. REFLECTING ADAM

(52 MINUTES REMAIN; USE 12 MINUTES IN THIS SECTION)

Ask a volunteer to read aloud Romans 5:12-14 from the *Jesus-Centered Bible* (p. 1177).

> Say: **The Apostle Paul, who wrote this letter to Christians in ancient Rome, makes some pretty strong claims in these verses. One of them is that Adam—and by extension, Eve, Adam's wife—are a *representation* of Jesus.**
>
> **We'll dig into exactly what that might mean, but first let's look at Adam and Eve's backstory so we can gain a new insight into who Jesus is and what he did for us.**

Ask one volunteer to read aloud Genesis 2:15-17 and another volunteer to read aloud Genesis 3:1-6 (pp. 6-7).

> Say: **These passages are familiar to many people who've been in church awhile. They're so familiar that it's easy to just gloss over what they tell us about Jesus and ourselves.**
>
> **In fact, most of us don't look for Jesus anywhere near the Garden of Eden; we may think he doesn't come on stage until the New Testament! But, according to Paul, there's something we can discover about Jesus in these passages.**

As a whole group, talk about what happened in the Garden:

❷ **Why do you think Adam and Eve gave in to the serpent's temptation? What motivated them to disregard God's instructions?**

Allow time for several comments. Then ask participants to again huddle up with their groups of four to discuss this question:

❷ **What are some instances you've seen of those same motivations playing out in our world today...and perhaps in your own life?**

After groups have had time to share, call their attention back to you with a one-minute warning. Once one minute has passed, move on to the next section.

3. RELATIONSHIPS IN PERIL

(40 MINUTES REMAIN; USE 10 MINUTES IN THIS SECTION)

Say: **Thanks for sharing in your small groups—and in our larger conversations, too. I'm glad we're exploring this together.**

Some things went seriously wrong when Adam and Eve disobeyed God. Among other consequences, three primary relationships were damaged and distorted.

Ask a volunteer to read aloud Genesis 3:7 in the *Jesus-Centered Bible* (p. 7).

Say: **The first relationship that took a hit was the relationship between Adam and Eve. From totally open and honest to shameful...that's a big leap.**

Ask a second volunteer to read aloud Genesis 3:8-11.

Ask the whole group to discuss:

❷ What relationship took a hit in this passage?

Allow several responses and then continue.

> Say: **So we've got Adam and Eve's disobedience hurting their relationship as a couple, and also their relationship with God. A third relationship was also damaged.**
>
> Read aloud Genesis 3:14-19, and then say: **Notice how the relationship between Adam and Eve and the rest of creation encountered a problem, too. Eve was sentenced to painful childbirth and relational challenges. Adam was burdened with the need to earn food by the sweat of his brow.**
>
> **As best I can tell, those consequences are still in play.**
>
> **The Hebrew word *adam* means "man." That implies that Adam—and Eve—are a representation of all people... including us. Their story is our story, too.**
>
> **In your small group of four, talk about this:**
>
> **❷ In what ways have you seen—or experienced— relationships broken as a result of disobeying God? What happened?**

Allow time for small groups of four to share. When a minute of time is left, gently interrupt to let them know to wrap up the conversation and focus on you in another 60 seconds.

4. SIN BY THE NUMBERS

(30 MINUTES REMAIN; USE 10 MINUTES IN THIS SECTION)

Say: **Adam and Eve's story turns out...poorly. But God gave their descendants a chance to make things right again.**

God rescued them from captivity in Egypt and led them toward a place they could call home, under the leadership of Moses. Among other places in the Bible, that journey is described in the book of Numbers.

Ask five volunteers to read aloud the first five paragraphs— one paragraph each—from the "Jesus in Numbers" essay on page 136 of the *Jesus-Centered Bible*.

Then ask participants to turn to page 153 in the *Jesus-Centered Bible* and silently read Numbers 14:1-4, 26-45. When it appears everyone has finished the passage, ask each person to find a partner and talk about this:

The Israelites chose to disobey God...with disastrous consequences.

❷ **Tell about a time you chose to disobey someone— your parents, a teacher, even God—and had to suffer consequences. What happened, and how did it turn out?**

Allow time for pairs to share.

5. ADAM AND JESUS

(20 MINUTES REMAIN; USE 3 MINUTES IN THIS SECTION)

Say: **Thank you for sharing your stories.**

Because none of us is perfect, it's not hard to think of times we've been disobedient. Disobedience seems to be part of our natural wiring.

But that wasn't the case with Adam and Eve—or Jesus. At least for a time, Adam and Eve chose to be faithful in loving and obeying God. It was a deliberate choice, and as long as they made that choice they were fine.

Jesus made the same choice—to love and obey his Father. But unlike Adam, Jesus never wavered. He was ever and always loving and obedient to his heavenly Father.

Both Adam and Jesus were the first of their kind. But through Adam the world encountered suffering and death. Through Jesus the world encountered life.

You and I are living both Adam's story and Jesus' story.

We sin and disobey God, and that's like Adam. But because of what Jesus has done for us, through his grace we can live his story of life, too.

Ask for a volunteer to read aloud Romans 5:15-19 (pp. 1177-1178).

6. HOPE IN JESUS

(17 MINUTES REMAIN; USE 7 MINUTES IN THIS SECTION)

Say: **Is Jesus the new Adam? Yes—they're both first of their kind. But they're very different. Through Adam sin entered the world. Through Jesus a new kind of life became possible.**

Have participants turn to page 7 in their *Jesus-Centered Bibles* and follow along as you read aloud the "Reframing Jesus" sidebar there.

Say: **Notice that the author uses war language. Jesus will "fight for humanity." He's "behind enemy lines." Jesus is clearly in a struggle to keep you spiritually safe and to have you for his own.**

A question for your group of four:

❷ **In what ways have you experienced Jesus fighting for you? Or haven't you ever felt that?**

Allow groups time for discussion. Then say: **Let's report back to the larger group. Is anyone willing to share with the whole group what you discussed in your group of four?**

7. FIGHTING THE FIGHT

(10 MINUTES REMAIN; USE 7 MINUTES IN THIS SECTION)

Say: **Jesus isn't the only one in a spiritual fight—you're in one, too. Regardless of whether you sense it, you're in the same struggle Adam was.**

You want to obey; you know that's the right and smart thing to do. But temptation is just so...tempting. Whether it's a piece of fruit in the Garden of Eden or a website you shouldn't visit or a tax deduction you shouldn't take, opportunities to fall short of faithfully following God are everywhere.

And, too often, we find them.

I'm not going to ask you to confess your darkest, most hidden sin—though if you want to, we can get together to have that conversation later. What I'd like you to do in your group of four is to pause to consider what helps you obey God.

What helps you be more like Jesus, the second Adam, than the original Adam? Maybe it's surrounding yourself with fellow believers, or worshipping often, or reading the Bible.

Whatever it is that helps you obey God, share that with your group of four. We can learn from each other and encourage one another—and that's a good thing to do!

Talk about this:

❓ What helps you obey God? Especially when you're facing some sort of temptation, what's helpful in resisting it?

Allow time for groups of four to talk.

8. BLESSINGS

(3 MINUTES REMAIN; USE 3 MINUTES IN THIS SECTION)

Say: **Thanks for sharing in your small group.**

Jesus was obedient and faithful...and we want to be, too. But when we fail, when we fall short, it can derail our relationship with Jesus. We begin hiding from him, sort of like Adam and Eve hid from God the Father in the Garden of Eden.

It's healthier to actually come to God, like King David did after he committed adultery. He confessed...and his confession touches the heart.

Ask participants to stand and to close their eyes and cup their hands together in front of them.

> Say: **I'm going to read aloud from David's confession found in Psalm 51. David realized he'd disobeyed God's will for his life, and he wanted to make things right with God. That's why he asked for forgiveness.**
>
> **The part of us that's like Adam—the rebellious, disobedient part—also needs forgiveness. As you listen to me read, let David's confession be yours as well.**

Read—slowly and deliberately—Psalm 51:1-12 (pp. 589-590). When you've finished, close with this prayer:

> **God, thank you for your love and forgiveness.**
>
> **We're a lot like Adam. We fall short. We fail. We sin.**
>
> **How wonderful that your grace and love can wash us clean.**
>
> **We thank you, God—and praise you.**
>
> **Amen.**

ABIDING IN JESUS

Experiment during the coming week with the spiritual practice of confession. Confession allows us to receive God's grace and mercy and experience forgiveness and healing. This week, take the challenge to share your weaknesses and failures with God and with another trusted person.

Here are some Scripture passages that can shape the practice of confession: Numbers 5:5-7; Psalm 32:1-5; James 5:16; 1 John 1:8-9.

Afterward, consider the following:

❓ Describe the costs and benefits of confession that you discovered.

_____

_____

_____

_____

_____

_____

❓ How can you make confession a regular practice to keep your relationship with Jesus open and honest?

_____

_____

_____

_____

_____

_____

SESSION 3:
JESUS—MAN ON A MISSION

SESSION SUMMARY

In this session you'll encounter Jesus as a man on a mission—a mission to fulfill the promise made to Abram generations before.

Ⓙ SUPPLIES NEEDED:

- A copy of the *Jesus-Centered Bible* for each person
- A deck of cards—each participant will need 3 playing cards
- A photocopy of the "Abiding in Jesus" take-home page for each person

---

1. GATHERING

(60 MINUTES REMAIN; USE 6 MINUTES IN THIS SECTION)

Greet participants and welcome them warmly.

Say: **Everyone, please stand. In a moment I'm going to send you on a mission and that's to shake the hand of everyone in the room. What makes this mission a bit tricky is that you don't know how long you've got to achieve the goal. It may be a few minutes, in which case you can take all the time you want to wander around and shake hands; or it may be just a few seconds, in which case...well, in which case you'd best gallop at full speed!**

If you have just a handful of people participating, allow only a few seconds. If you've got 20 or more people in the room, take a bit more time.

Ready to get shaking? Go!

Allow time for shaking hands. When you're ready to stop, say loudly: **Freeze! Everyone stop where you are!**

Ask participants to pair up with the person whose hand they're shaking. Pair up people who are between shakes. You can always join in to make an even number of people.

Say: **Briefly tell your partner your name and something important you're doing lately. As for me...**

Very briefly share something you've been doing lately that you consider important.

Say: **That's a mission I'm on. What about you? Tell your partner something you're doing lately that you take seriously—it's important to you.**

Allow time for partners to share. Then thank them for sharing and ask that each pair find another pair to form a group of four people. Ask the groups of four to find a place to sit so they can talk together easily.

2. CARD TOWERS

(54 MINUTES REMAIN; USE 6 MINUTES IN THIS SECTION)

Say: **I've got a mission for you and it's this: Build a tower.**

Give each person three playing cards.

Say: **Some rules: You'll build a card tower but you can't stick cards together in any way or bend cards. As you build a tower, you have to work together—taking turns placing cards to create your structure. It's okay if two of you place cards at the same time, but keep in mind this is a *group* effort.**

You'll have up to three minutes to create your skyscraper. Ready? Pick a spot to build; in 60 seconds I'll start the clock on construction.

After 60 seconds—less if each group quickly picks a spot to build—say: **Go!**

Give updates every 30 seconds and count down the last 15 seconds. When three minutes have passed, say: **That's it! Let's take a look at what you built.**

Compliment all structures as you look at them. Then ask groups to knock down their towers and collect the cards.

3. CARD TOWERS DEBRIEF

(48 MINUTES REMAIN; USE 5 MINUTES IN THIS SECTION)

Say: **A question for us as a whole group:**

❓ **What did it take to be a good team member as you worked on towers?**

Allow several responses, and then move on to the following question:

❓ **Let's say there was a million-dollar prize for building the tallest tower. In what ways would that have changed how you approached this mission—or wouldn't it have mattered?**

Allow several responses.

4. JESUS ON A MISSION

(43 MINUTES REMAIN; USE 5 MINUTES IN THIS SECTION)

Say: **Thanks for sharing your thoughts. And just so we're clear: No million dollars was at stake here. You couldn't even keep the cards.**

It's not news to most Christians that when Jesus was on earth he was on a mission—one he took very seriously. Just out of curiosity, what do you think that mission was?

Allow several suggestions.

Say: **Thanks for sharing.**

According to the Bible, Jesus was on *several* missions. He was out to seek and save the lost (Luke 19:10). He came to serve (Mark 10:45). He came so we could have an abundant life (John 10:10). He came to reveal the Father (Matthew 11:27), to preach (Luke 4:43), and to destroy the works of the devil (1 John 3:8). Lots of missions—and he took them all seriously.

But Jesus' overarching mission, which included all these we've mentioned, was to fulfill a promise. A promise made centuries before he arrived on the scene in Palestine.

Ask a volunteer to read aloud Genesis 12:2 (p.15). Then read aloud the Blue Explanation Box at the bottom of page 15.

Say: **Notice the stack of promises made to Abram: becoming famous, having a great nation borne from his family, becoming a blessing to others. But the big one—that all the families on earth will be blessed through Abram— that's something Abram didn't live to see come to pass.**

None of Abram's descendants saw it happen...until the family tree sprouted Jesus, the Messiah.

Ask a volunteer to read aloud Matthew 1:1-2, 16 (p. 999) and another volunteer to read the "Jesus in Matthew" essay on page 998.

Say: **When Jesus arrived he did so as a man on a mission, and that primary mission was to become that promised blessing to all families everywhere.**

5. JESUS A BLESSING?

(38 MINUTES REMAIN; USE 10 MINUTES IN THIS SECTION)

Ask participants to gather again in their groups of four—the same people with whom they built skyscrapers.

Say: **Jesus came to fulfill a promise: to be a blessing to people everywhere...which would include us. So let's talk about how he did in fulfilling that mission.**

In your small group, talk about this:

❷ **In what ways has Jesus blessed you?**

Allow time for groups to talk.

Say: **There's what Jesus did while he was here on earth— his teachings and what he did on the cross and his resurrection. Those were huge blessings that allow us to have a relationship with God.**

But was that all Jesus came to do? Bless everyone once, and then sort of slide off into retirement? Or is he blessing us currently? Is he in a present-tense relationship with us?

In your small group, please talk about this:

❓ In what ways—at home, work, or other places in your life—is Jesus currently blessing you? How do you know it's him at work in your life?

Allow time for groups to talk, and then ask if anyone is willing to share with the larger group what he or she shared in the small group. In what ways is Jesus currently providing blessings—and how does the person who's sharing know that it's Jesus at work?

6. TEAM JESUS

(28 MINUTES REMAIN; USE 10 MINUTES IN THIS SECTION)

Say: **Thank you for sharing. It's good to remember that Jesus wasn't just a man on a mission; he's a man *still* on a mission. And more than a man at that!**

And he's not alone in the mission of being a blessing to others. As his followers, we've inherited the same expectation that was given to Abram: We're blessed so we can be a blessing to others.

Which leads to two questions: What does it take to be a member of Team Jesus? And how might we also bless others?

Let's look at the first question: What does it take to be a member of the team? Writing in the book of Romans, Paul offers a pretty good answer in chapter 4.

Ask participants to turn to page 1176 in their *Jesus-Centered Bibles* and to follow along as a volunteer reads aloud Romans 4:1-5, 13-17, 23-25.

Say: **What does it take to be a part of this mission team with Jesus? Faith in him. All the good stuff we do is nice, but it's no substitute for faith in God.**

Ask participants to form pairs, and then continue:

In a moment I'll ask you to deliver a quick State of the Union Address concerning your faith. Our faith can ebb and flow, sometimes rock solid and other times less so.

I'll ask you to rate your faith on a scale from 1 to 10. If it's a 10, you have a rock-solid confidence that Jesus is walking with you and you're following him well. If you rank your faith a 1, you might wonder if Jesus is out there anywhere—you feel distant and out of touch.

You might be feeling like a 10...or a 1...or somewhere in between. As for me, this week I feel like a...

Very briefly share how you'd rank your faith and why. Model the transparency you hope is shared in conversations that will soon follow.

❓ **How about you? Are you currently feeling like a 10... or a 1...or somewhere in between? And why? Take a few minutes to share as partners.**

Allow time for partners to share; then call attention back to yourself.

7. PRAYER

(18 MINUTES REMAIN; USE 2 MINUTES IN THIS SECTION)

Say: **Thanks for sharing together. Because we're all members of the team, let's do this: Let's pray for one another.**

Maybe you said you were a 10 this week—great! But next week is coming, and it has challenges in it that may rock your world and your faith. We need one another's support as we live out our faith in the world, so let's provide some support in prayer.

Please exchange *Jesus-Centered Bibles* with your partner.

Pause as partners do as you've asked. Then continue.

Say: **Now please silently pray for your partner—for your partner's life and faith. Thank Jesus for your partner, and ask Jesus to draw close as your partner deals with all that life brings his or her way. Pray silently for 60 seconds, and then I'll close.**

After 60 seconds, pray:

Thank you, Lord, for your blessings...for the blessing our partner is to us. Be with the person whose Bible we hold. Amen.

After this prayer, have everyone return the Bibles to their owners.

8. MISSION FEEDBACK

(16 MINUTES REMAIN; USE 7 MINUTES IN THIS SECTION)

Say: **Thank you. Now let's talk about that second question: How can we be a blessing to others?**

Form up with your skyscraper group again, and talk about this:

❓ **In what ways are you blessing others? And what gets in the way of your being even more of a blessing?**

Allow time for groups of four to talk, and then ask if volunteers are willing to share with the larger group what they identified as obstacles to being even more of a blessing.

Allow several responses.

9. STAYING ON MISSION

(11 MINUTES REMAIN; USE 8 MINUTES IN THIS SECTION)

Say: **Good news! Just like Abram, our role in Jesus' mission doesn't depend on us always perfectly performing our part.**

We're here because of his grace, and our faith. But since we're here, let's do the best we can to stay on mission.

I'm curious: If our mission is to both follow Jesus and bless others, what have you found helpful in doing that? In your skyscraper group of four, talk about this:

❓ **What's helped you follow Jesus and bless others?**

Allow time for groups to talk. Then ask: **Anyone willing to share with the whole group what you talked about? Given that none of us is perfect, what helps you stay on mission?**

Allow several responses.

10. CLOSING PRAYER

(3 MINUTES REMAIN; USE 3 MINUTES IN THIS SECTION)

Say: **Thanks for sharing from your experience. And thanks for praying for one another. Jesus was—and is—on a mission, and we're privileged to be included on the team he's called to accomplish it.**

Let's close our time together by thanking him for that, and asking for his help in faithfully following and serving him.

I'll open a prayer and then, when everyone who wants to pray aloud has done so, I'll close.

Jesus, thank you for the honor of following and serving you. Thanks for calling us, and for loving us. Please hear our prayers.

Pause as long as necessary to allow all who wish to pray aloud to do so; then close the prayer time: **We love you, Jesus. Amen.**

ABIDING IN JESUS

"Mission drift" is the danger of a person or group gradually losing sight of their original vision and mission. This can happen to Christians and churches, too.

One biblical practice that has helped God's people remember and stay true to God's mission is the Jewish Passover and its Christian counterpart, Communion. If you'd like to go deeper into this practice, do the following during the coming week:

- Read Exodus 12:1-14 and the Blue Explanation Box at the bottom of page 70.

- Read Numbers 9:1-5 and the "Reframing Jesus" sidebar on page 148.

- Read Luke 22:7-20 (p. 1100). Write down everything that this passage tells you about Jesus' love for his followers and his commitment to God's mission.

- Consider how rituals and customs like Communion help you remember what God has done for you in the past and today.

SESSION 4:
JESUS ON EARTH

SESSION SUMMARY

During this session you'll discover the meaning behind some of Jesus' titles that reveal the true nature of his ministry on earth. You'll also explore ways to carry on Jesus' ministry by following him more closely.

Ⓙ SUPPLIES NEEDED:

- A copy of the *Jesus-Centered Bible* for each person
- A photocopy of the "Abiding in Jesus" take-home page for each person

---

1. GATHERING

(60 MINUTES REMAIN; USE 6 MINUTES IN THIS SECTION)

Greet participants and welcome them warmly.

Say: **Let's get to know each other a bit better. Everyone find a partner, please—if at all possible, partner with someone you didn't come here with today.**

Allow time for participants to pair up, and then continue.

In a few moments, I'm going to ask you to tell your partner about your family's ethnic or national origins and what, if anything, your name means. For instance, you might say, "My great-great grandparents came to New York City from Italy in the early 1900s, and I have no idea what my name means," or "My family is originally from Senegal in West Africa, and my name means 'Distant Hills.'"

As for me...

Briefly share about your origins and what, if anything, your name means.

Say: **Your turn now. Tell your partner what you know.**

Allow time for pairs to do as you've asked, and then continue.

Say: **Thanks for sharing.**

2. CITIZENSHIP

(54 MINUTES REMAIN; USE 5 MINUTES IN THIS SECTION)

Say: **Here's something for you to ponder with your partner: Immigration has been in the news a lot the past few years. Suppose that, for whatever reason, you had to permanently leave this country and immigrate to another country. Discuss this with your partner:**

❷ **What country would you choose to live in, and why?**

Allow time for pairs to share, and then continue.

Say: **In some ways, Christians have already immigrated. They—we—belong to not just the nation where we're living but also to a kingdom that's ruled by a King, one who's unlike any other king.**

Let's look into what the Bible says about kings in general.

3. GOD'S KING

(49 MINUTES REMAIN; USE 10 MINUTES IN THIS SECTION)

Say: **We're going to read a coronation psalm, which is**

a song that was sung when a new king was crowned in ancient Israel.

Because none of us has actually been in ancient Israel to be at a coronation, here's a little inside information to help the psalm make sense:

Kings were anointed with olive oil when they came to the throne. And because the Hebrew word for "anointed one" is *messiah*, the word "king" = "messiah."

Kings were believed to have an especially close relationship to God, like that of father and son.

Kings represented the entire nation before God, and the people looked to the king for godly leadership. So when God looked at the king, God saw Israel. When the people looked at the king, they saw God.

Ask a volunteer to read aloud Psalm 2:1-7 (p. 561) while everyone else follows along in the *Jesus-Centered Bible.*

When the reader finishes, ask each pair to partner up with another pair to form a group of four. Ask the groups of four to discuss:

❷ How safe and secure would you feel living in a country that had a king like the one described in this psalm? Why?

Allow time for groups of four to share, and then continue. Say: **Here's a question we can answer as a whole group:**

❷ What might be some possible drawbacks to living under this kind of king?

Allow several responses.

Say: **Thanks for placing yourself in the sandals of an ancient Israelite. There's a reason that's significant today... so let's find out why.**

4. KING JESUS

(39 MINUTES REMAIN; USE 12 MINUTES IN THIS SECTION)

Ask three volunteers to read aloud the "Reframing Jesus" sidebar on page 562 of the *Jesus-Centered Bible*, one paragraph each, while other participants follow along in their Bibles.

Say: **Let's jump ahead almost a thousand years from the time Psalm 2 was sung aloud outside Jerusalem to another, very different, coronation.**

Ask a volunteer to read aloud Matthew 3:13-17 (p. 1001).

Say: **Did you catch the words that Jesus heard from heaven? "My Son," the same words ancient kings heard. And like those kings, Jesus was also anointed, but by the Spirit of God instead of oil.**

Watching from the riverbanks that day, the average observer may have been baffled by this anointing. It wasn't like God hadn't picked unusual kings before—David was a young shepherd when chosen to be king. But Jesus? A carpenter from Nazareth? Perhaps there was some doubt about Jesus being king.

Which leads me to a question for us: In what ways have we doubted Jesus as our king? Please know there's no condemnation coming along with this question. The truth is that we've all had times in our lives—including after we became Jesus-followers—when our attitudes and actions didn't exactly trumpet that we were citizens of Jesus' kingdom.

Or maybe we've had times when life hit us with hard things and that prompted us to wonder for a time if Jesus was really there and in charge. Maybe we wonder that today.

Again, there's no shame in doubt. But there is danger if we don't talk about our doubts and instead let them fester in the darkness. When we bring doubts into the light, we can deal with them.

One time that I found myself doubting that Jesus was king— at least king of my world—was when…

Briefly share a time you experienced doubt. Model the sort of transparency and sharing you hope happens in groups of four.

Say: **That's how doubt about King Jesus played out in my world…how about you?**

In your group of four, talk about this:

❓ **When have you questioned or doubted Jesus—or haven't you had that experience? If you have experienced doubt, what was that experience like?**

Allow time for groups of four to share.

5. DOUBT PRAYER

(27 MINUTES REMAIN; USE 1 MINUTE IN THIS SECTION)

Say: **Thank you for sharing in your small group. Maybe it was a bit scary admitting that at times you've experienced doubt. But if that's the case, you're in excellent company.**

Some of Jesus' closest followers doubted him now and then. Even John the Baptist sent someone to double-check if Jesus was really the Messiah—and John had been there at Jesus' coronation! (Matthew 3:13-17; 11:2-3)

Doubt isn't the end of faith; it's an opportunity to renew a relationship with Jesus and to grow deeper in him.

In your group of four, please hold hands as I pray for you.

Pause to allow groups to do as you've asked.

Say: **God, thank you for your love for us.**

Thank you that it's big and deep enough for us to sometimes doubt you.

Help us love you more deeply and know you better, as you love and know us.

Move us past our doubts. And thank you for our King.

Amen.

6. CITIZENSHIP AFFIRMATION

(26 MINUTES REMAIN; USE 9 MINUTES IN THIS SECTION)

Say: **We get lots of reminders that we're citizens of our nation. We pay taxes. We salute the flag. We're reminded in a hundred ways that this is where we live. Even if our nationality is elsewhere, we're reminded where we're from and who we are.**

But it's easy to forget our citizenship in the kingdom of God—and that's our most important citizenship. Yes, we owe a great deal to our country, but ultimately it's King Jesus who deserves our highest allegiance. He's given us our true identity.

Just as Jesus' identity and mission was confirmed at his coronation in the River Jordan, he confirms our identity and mission.

Ask a volunteer to read aloud Romans 8:15-17a (p. 1180).

Say: **When we identify ourselves with Jesus, God gives us his Spirit and says to us, "You are my dear, dear child; I'm delighted with you."**

Let's remind each other of that right now. Find a partner, please.

Allow a moment for participants to find partners.

Say: **In a moment I'll ask you to say something to your partner, and it's this...**

Move to where you're seated and facing someone. Look that person in the eye and take his or her hands. Say: **"_____ [Name], you are God's dear [son or daughter]. God is delighted in you."**

Repeat what you said several times, and then speak to the whole group.

Say: **Move your chairs, or stand, so you're directly facing your partner. Look each other in the eye and hold hands, or shake hands—really, trust me on this—as you take turns saying what I said back and forth at least four times. Let the truth of those words sink deeply into your heart; they're words you don't often hear.**

Allow partners time to do as you've asked. Then ask the whole group:

❷ **What was it like to hear those words of blessing? How easy or hard is it for you to believe them, and why?**

Allow several responses.

7. KING JESUS' JOB EVALUATION

(17 MINUTES REMAIN; USE 8 MINUTES IN THIS SECTION)

Thank participants for sharing both those words of blessing and their responses to your question.

Say: **When Jesus stepped into his role as God's anointed king—Messiah—his relationship with God wasn't just one of privilege. He took on some responsibilities for the citizens of his kingdom—and that would be the whole world, including us.**

Let's see how the prophet Isaiah described that job.

Ask everyone to read to themselves Isaiah 61:1-3 (p. 761), plus the Blue Explanation Box at the bottom of that page.

Then ask small groups of four to discuss:

❷ **Given that job description, how did you see Jesus fulfilling it in the Bible?**

❷ **And how do you see him fulfilling it today?**

After groups of four have had time to discuss this, ask them to report back to the whole group what they talked about.

Allow several responses.

8. STILL TO GO

(9 MINUTES REMAIN; USE 5 MINUTES IN THIS SECTION)

Say: **Thank you for sharing your thoughts.**

Here's the thing about being the king: You don't do everything yourself in your kingdom; that's why you've got subjects. If Jesus is our King and we're his subjects, it stands to reason that we've got some stuff to do.

When Jesus was visiting Nazareth, he declared both who he was and what he'd come to do. Let's take a moment to join him.

Ask a volunteer to read aloud Luke 4:14-21 (p. 1071).

Say: **Something for us to talk about as a whole group:**

❷ **Which, if any, of Jesus' goals remain incomplete? How might we be able to participate in our King's ongoing mission?**

Allow several responses.

9. CLOSE TO THE KING

(4 MINUTES REMAIN; USE 4 MINUTES IN THIS SECTION)

Say: **Thank you for sharing your thoughts and insights.**

Being a participant in Jesus' mission can turn into a big to-do list of "shoulds" if we're not careful. That's a common trap and one that sucks the joy out of being a follower of Jesus.

The best way to live as one of Jesus' loyal subjects is to keep a close relationship with him. As a whole group let's offer each other some encouragement and insight as we wrap up. Let's suggest ways to stay close to the King.

Ask the whole group:

❷ **What are ways that you draw close to Jesus? Maybe it's a Bible study or a nature walk. Maybe it's singing, dancing, or doodling. What helps you draw close to Jesus?**

Allow several responses. Dig deeper if someone gives a generic response like "Read the Bible." Ask, "What part of the Bible? What are you looking for? What do you think about as you're reading?"

ABIDING IN JESUS

Here are some practices to "test drive" in the next week to help you keep close to Jesus:

- Read one of the Gospels—Matthew, Mark, Luke, or John—for the clearest description of Jesus' words and actions about the kingdom of God.

- Read at least one Bible story about Jesus multiple times. Each time use one of your five senses to imagine being part of the story:

  1. One time imagine what you would see.

  2. Another time imagine what you would hear (read dialogue aloud).

  3. Think about the smells you would encounter.

  4. Imagine the tastes of any food or drink in the story.

  5. What would your sense of touch tell you? Sense the breeze, the clothes, the vases and pots, the buildings, and so on.

_____

_____

_____

_____

_____

_____

_____

SESSION 5:
SAVIOR JESUS

SESSION SUMMARY
In this session you'll encounter Jesus as Savior, exploring what he meant when describing himself as "Son of Man."

> **(J.) SUPPLIES NEEDED:**
> - A copy of the *Jesus-Centered Bible* for each person
> - A photocopy of the "Abiding in Jesus" take-home page for each person

1. GATHERING

(60 MINUTES REMAIN; USE 8 MINUTES IN THIS SECTION)

Greet participants and welcome them warmly. Ask participants to form small groups of four and to sit so they can comfortably talk with their small group.

Say: **Everyone in this room has needed help to get out of a tight spot. Maybe mom or dad loaned you money so you could make rent a time or two, or perhaps when you were young someone came to your rescue when a bully singled you out for a beat down.**

In a moment I'll ask you to share about a time someone had to bail you out of a difficult situation...maybe by literally posting your bail. As for me, one time that happened was when...

Briefly tell about a time you needed to be bailed out of a problem. Describe what the situation was and who came to your rescue.

Say: **That's my story, and I'm hoping you'll share yours in your small group. Talk about this, please:**

❓ **Tell about a time you were bailed out of a tough situation. What was the situation, and who came to your rescue?**

Allow time for small groups to share stories. When about a minute of time is left for sharing, say: **You have about a minute left to share.** This lets small groups know that if there's someone who hasn't yet had the chance to speak, it's time to shift to that person.

2. SHORT OF BREATH

(52 MINUTES REMAIN; USE 4 MINUTES IN THIS SECTION)

Say: **Thanks for sharing your stories! I'd like us to do a little experiment together.**

First, imagine you're a dashing international spy who regularly saves the world. You're on a huge yacht and just discovered a bomb is attached to the hull under it. There's no time for scuba gear so you'll have to dive overboard, swim past huge, spinning propellers, subdue a dozen underwater ninjas, and carefully disarm the bomb.

All while holding your breath.

So take a few deep breaths to prepare. In...and out. In... fill your lungs so you get as much oxygen as possible...and out.

When I give you the signal, please take a deep breath and hold it until you either save the ship or have to exhale. But don't pass out!

Ready? Take a deep breath to hold...now.

Note: *Read this with enthusiasm and make it fun—it will take almost two minutes to go through the story, which means most participants will have taken a new breath or be red-faced by the time you finish.*

Okay, you're under the boat, you're past the ninjas, and you need to find the bomb. No problem—you've been trained where to look. It's always under the most vulnerable portion of the hull, so you swim toward that critical spot and there it is.

But as you study the bomb's control panel, your body is now noticing your oxygen supply is cut off and your chest is starting to ache.

There's a growing sense of discomfort as carbon dioxide builds up in your system. But there's a boat to save, so you look at the panel and realize there's an access code needed.

That *is* a problem because the code could be anything and you're distracted: your body desperately wants a breath. Your heart rate is rising...your diaphragm may be starting to convulse.

The evil genius who planted the bomb was born in January, so there's likely a "1" in there somewhere...but what else might give you a clue? You pull out your special underwater spy phone and pull up Spy Central to see what it can tell you...

Which is plenty—turns out this sort of bomb doesn't need an access code, so you can push any four buttons to bypass the countdown.

But your muscles are now quivering, so it's hard to hit any button at all. And you're distracted. If you could just take a breath, release the CO_2, take in fresh oxygen! It's hard to concentrate, which is unfortunate because here comes...a shark!

Which you know won't get you, because you have shark repellent built right into your spy shoes. Sure enough, the shark takes a run at you and suddenly veers off. You're safe, so you focus back—sort of—on the control panel.

You know you can do this. You've been trained for it. You have all the information you need. This is why you went to spy school, where you graduated at the top of your class. You've memorized the blueprints for every inch of this yacht, and you know whether to cut the green or red wire when defusing bombs. You know your stuff.

And that's what you're thinking as you black out and the boat blows up.

Okay, everyone—take a breath!

3. SHORT-OF-BREATH DEBRIEF

(48 MINUTES REMAIN; USE 3 MINUTES IN THIS SECTION)

Say: **Thanks for being good sports about that activity. As you catch your breath, let's talk—or try to talk—about something as a whole group.**

❷ **What went wrong? You had a ton of information—all the information you needed. Why didn't you complete the mission and save yourself and others? What were you lacking?**

Allow several responses.

4. SAVED BY A SNAKE

(45 MINUTES REMAIN; USE 12 MINUTES IN THIS SECTION)

Say: **Whatever else you needed, you needed air. All the information in the world can't help you if you're out of air.**

Sometimes, when we need saving, we need something very specific. That may have been true in the story you told earlier, and it's certainly true for those of us who are imperfect people. We don't need more information about how to be good; our shaping up a bit doesn't take care of our sins.

We need forgiveness—and a *Savior*. That's what's really needed.

Today we're exploring how Jesus is that Savior we need.

Ask everyone to follow along in their *Jesus-Centered Bibles* as you read aloud Numbers 21:4-7 (p. 162).

When you finish reading, ask the group this penetrating question:

An infestation of venomous snakes seems like a pretty severe reaction to complaints about the food. And yet, the people didn't blame God for the snakes; they accepted the snakes as the just consequence of their rebellion. So, there had to be a deeper issue behind these verses.

❓ **What relational tensions do you think lay behind the complaints?**

Take a few responses from the group—about four minutes max. Be sure to thank and affirm those who shared before moving on to this follow-up question, taking no more than another four minutes:

❓ How accurately do you think this represents all of us humans? Any examples come to mind?

After several responses have been offered, go a little deeper by saying this:

It's painfully obvious that we humans do a lot of damage to our relationships with God and each other, and many times suffer the consequences. But, as this story from Numbers shows, God goes the extra mile to save us from ourselves.

Ask a volunteer to read aloud Numbers 21:8-9. Then say: **Generally, snakes have a nasty reputation in the Bible. But here, the bronze snake becomes a source of healing— undoing what the real, live snakes did.**

Other ancient cultures saw healing powers in snakes, but they had to recite mysterious formulas or go through a series of magical actions. God didn't require any of that; the people only had to look to God's remedy.

❓ What does this say about God's love and mercy for people—even complaining, rebellious people?

Take a few minutes for the group to discuss God's response to the snake attacks.

5. JESUS THE HEALER

(33 MINUTES REMAIN; USE 10 MINUTES IN THIS SECTION)

Say: **Most likely, no one here has suffered from a venomous snake bite. (If you have, we're so glad to have you here with us!)**

However, we've all been bitten by the evil of sin in the world, either by hurting other people or by being hurt. Maybe both.

Thankfully, God has provided a remedy for that, too. Let's check it out.

Ask the group to gather again into their groups of four and read the "Reframing Jesus" sidebar on page 162 and John 3:13-17 (p. 1110). When they have finished reading, ask the groups to discuss this question:

❷ Jesus compares himself to the bronze snake in the Old Testament and says that those who believe in him will have eternal life. How is believing in him like—or unlike— looking at the bronze snake for healing?

Give the groups about four minutes to discuss this question. After three minutes, gently announce that they have one minute left. When that last minute is up, ask the group members to share their responses to this next question:

❷ How have you experienced healing of some kind as a result of believing in Jesus? Take a few minutes to share with the friends in your small group.

After three minutes, alert the groups to take one more minute to share their stories with each other. Then transition to the next part of this Bible study.

Say: **Unfortunately, most of Jesus' contemporaries struggled to see him as their savior because their idea of a savior was as a political or military hero. That's true even though key prophecies indicated the Savior would be a very different kind of hero.**

6. SUFFERING SAVIOR

(23 MINUTES REMAIN; USE 10 MINUTES IN THIS SECTION)

Ask a volunteer to read aloud Isaiah 53:4-8 (p. 753).
Then ask another volunteer to read the "Reframing Jesus"
sidebar on page 754.

Say: **Some people missed Jesus for who he was—their
Savior—because of faulty expectations of Jesus. In your
group of four, please talk about this:**

❓ **What faulty expectations of Jesus do you see in the world
today? Expectations that keep people from seeing Jesus as
a Savior?**

Allow groups three minutes to discuss the question, giving a
one-minute warning when time is about up. After you draw
attention back to yourself, continue.

Say: **Is anyone willing to share with the whole group what
you talked about in your small group?**

Allow several responses.

Say: **Thanks for sharing. Isaiah's vision of a suffering
Savior has been difficult for some people to accept.
Sometimes it takes another person to point out some truths
about Jesus that we can't see. Here's a case in point...**

7. GOOD NEWS ABOUT JESUS

(13 MINUTES REMAIN; USE 13 MINUTES IN THIS SECTION)

Ask for four volunteers to help you read aloud Acts 8:26-35
(p. 1146). The volunteers will need to decide what part

they will read: 1) the angel of the Lord, 2) the Holy Spirit, 3) Philip, 4) the Ethiopian official. You'll read the narrator's lines.

When you and your readers have read the passage, ask participants to talk about the questions below in their groups of four. Allow about four minutes for each set of questions, remembering to give a one-minute warning for each.

❓ Has another person shown you a new insight about Jesus? What was that insight? Did it seem at the time to be good news?

❓ Philip was one of Jesus' original followers who had been with him until the end, and even after Jesus' resurrection. So he knew something about Jesus that the Ethiopian could not know. How do you see yourself and other Christians as today's "Philips"?

When time is up, ask for two or three groups to share with the entire group a brief summary of their discussion of the second question.

Thank the groups for sharing, and then close the session by praying aloud this prayer:

Dear God: We have been saved by the gift of your Son, Jesus. We can never thank you enough for that wonderful and costly gift. But still, thank you. Help us to live right now—in our daily lives—the eternal life you have given us.

And when we have the chance to tell others about you, give us the wisdom and the words to do so with the same love and mercy that you have shown us.

Amen.

ABIDING IN JESUS

Want to explore more about Jesus as Savior? Read the Blue Explanation Box (Isaiah 53) on page 753, followed by 2 Corinthians 5:11-21 (p. 1210).

The Jesus Question on page 1210 will guide you in deeper personal reflection on Jesus as Savior and your role as an agent of reconciliation.

_____

_____

_____

_____

_____

_____

_____

_____

_____

_____

_____

_____

_____

_____

_____

_____

_____

SESSION 6:
CORNERSTONE JESUS

SESSION SUMMARY

In this session you'll encounter Jesus as the founder and sustainer of the church—the worldwide group of people who call themselves Christians. You'll also explore your place and role in that group.

Ⓙ SUPPLIES NEEDED:

- A copy of the *Jesus-Centered Bible* for each person

- Assorted play building blocks, 4 pieces per person

- A photocopy of the "Abiding in Jesus" take-home page for each person

1. GATHERING

(60 MINUTES REMAIN; USE 10 MINUTES IN THIS SECTION)

Warmly greet and welcome everyone to this session. Then ask people to form small groups of four.

Say: **Get to know the people in your small group by discovering what other groups they belong to. Tell each other what groups, clubs, and organizations you currently belong to.**

I'm thinking of groups that have some degree of structure: fees, pledges, official leaders, rituals, secret handshakes, a newsletter, a regular meeting time, and so on. Extra points if you have a membership card or some sort of club ID with you.

I'll start by sharing a quick list of groups I'm a part of...

Quickly list some groups to which you belong—the longer the list, the better.

Say: **Your turn. Let's find out where the people in our small groups hang out when they're not here.**

Allow time for groups to talk. When there's one minute left for discussion, Say: **Take another minute to wrap up your conversation.** This lets groups know that if someone in the group hasn't yet spoken, it's time to give that person a turn to speak.

Say: **Thanks for sharing in your group. Now, in your small group, please talk about this:**

❷ **Of the groups you listed, which are most meaningful or significant in your life? Which groups are you least likely to ever leave—and why are you so committed to those groups?**

Allow time for groups to share; then draw attention back to yourself and continue.

Say: **We all long to belong somewhere. A good deal of our identity comes from the people with whom we live, work, and play. When we follow Jesus and belong to him, we don't do it alone. We become part of a movement with billions of other people who've also chosen to belong to Jesus.**

Let's dig into that.

2. JESUS AS CORNERSTONE

(50 MINUTES REMAIN; USE 8 MINUTES IN THIS SECTION)

Ask a volunteer to read aloud Isaiah 28:16 (p. 726) while everyone else follows along. Then ask the whole group this question:

❓ Given what you know about architecture and building, how would you say the function of a cornerstone differs from the function of a roof or window?

Allow several answers.

Say: **Thanks for your architectural input!**

These days, cornerstones are often ceremonial spots to place time capsules, but back in the day a cornerstone was the first stone placed in a masonry foundation. The rest of the stones were situated in reference to the cornerstone, so it determined the rest of the structure.

Isaiah wasn't talking about a cornerstone in a building in the verse we read, but rather another sort of cornerstone.

Ask a volunteer to read aloud the Blue Explanation Box on page 726, and then follow the link and ask a volunteer to read aloud Ephesians 2:19-22 (p. 1228).

Ask participants to re-form their groups of four.

Say: **In your small group, talk about this:**

❓ In this passage, the image of a cornerstone is applied to Jesus. In what ways do you think that's appropriate—or inappropriate?

After several minutes of discussion, give a one-minute warning.

Say: **I'd love to hear what you talked about in your small groups. Anyone willing to share with the larger group what you discussed? In what ways is Jesus a cornerstone—or not?**

Allow several responses.

3. CORNERSTONE CONNECTIONS

(42 MINUTES REMAIN; USE 10 MINUTES IN THIS SECTION)

Say: **Thank you for your insights!**

One place Jesus is a cornerstone is the church. That's what Paul was describing in the Ephesians passage. Without Jesus, the church is just one more social club. With Jesus, it's God's kingdom on earth. Jesus makes all the difference.

Let's talk about our experiences in church—and how connected we feel to the church's cornerstone, Jesus.

In your group of four, talk about this:

❓ **Tell about a time you felt very connected to Jesus. What part—if any—did the church play in that situation?**

Allow groups time to talk, and then continue.

Say: **Thanks for sharing. Here's another question for your group of four to consider:**

❓ **Paul used a lot of images to describe how Christians relate to God and one another: as citizens, as family, as a house, and as a temple. Which of those images best describes how you feel about your connections in church? Why do you answer as you do?**

Allow groups of four time to talk.

4. CONNECTION PRAYERS

(32 MINUTES REMAIN; USE 1 MINUTE IN THIS SECTION)

Thank small groups for sharing, and then say:

Not everyone feels as if they fully belong in Jesus' community of faith. Even people who feel a sense of belonging sometimes feel closer at one time than another time. I'd like to pause to pray for all who sometimes wonder if they're fully welcome in the church.

Lord Jesus, thank you for creating a people for yourself, people called to worship and minister in your name. Thank you for inviting us to be among those people, not because of anything we've done to earn or deserve it, but because you love us and want us to be in close relationship with you and with each other.

For those who don't feel as if they belong, send your Holy Spirit to remind them of your love and your invitation to be part of the church. For those who do feel they belong, give them open hearts and minds, and remind them to offer the same hospitality they've received.

Amen.

5. CORNERSTONE CONCERNS

(31 MINUTES REMAIN; USE 10 MINUTES IN THIS SECTION)

Say to the whole group:

Jesus may be a perfect cornerstone for the church, but somewhere along the way the rest of the building has at times gotten...a bit off-kilter.

That is, the church's reputation has been tarnished—often by church members.

This really isn't a new problem. Every now and then God has to remind us who we are. The Old Testament prophet Malachi dealt with these issues in his time.

Ask a volunteer to read aloud the "Jesus in Malachi" essay on page 990. Then ask another volunteer to read aloud Malachi 3:1, 16-18 (pp. 992 and 994).

Say: **Clearly God's people had issues back in Malachi's time. They shorted God with offerings. They didn't always treat each other or people who were powerless well.**

Yet consider the standard that's set in Malachi 3:16: We're to fear the Lord and always think about the honor of his name. That is, ever and always we're called to respect God and bring honor to him in what we think, say, and do.

A tall order, but there are examples of God's people honoring God's name together. As a whole group, let's list some of the ways that's happening across the globe and in our own town.

Allow several group responses.

Say: **Thanks. Now, in your group of four, please do this:**

❷ **Describe ways you're bringing honor to God's name. How is that playing out in your life...or isn't it?**

6. LIVING STONES

(21 MINUTES REMAIN; USE 10 MINUTES IN THIS SECTION)

Ask a volunteer to read aloud 1 Peter 2:4-10 (p. 1298) while the rest of the group follows along in their *Jesus-Centered Bibles*.

Then ask small groups of four to huddle up and again review 1 Peter 2:4-10 (p. 1298), looking for key words, phrases, or concepts that describe qualifications for gaining membership in God's chosen people.

After a few minutes, ask small groups to discuss:

❷ How do you feel about membership in God's people being a matter of God's gift of mercy, nothing else required? Why?

Allow time for small groups to discuss the question, and then move along to the following discussion question:

❷ Peter identifies Jesus as a stone that makes people stumble and fall. In what ways have you seen that be true—or not?

When about a minute is left for discussion, give a one-minute warning.

7. BUILDING BLOCKS

(11 MINUTES REMAIN; USE 7 MINUTES IN THIS SECTION)

Give each person four pieces from a play building block set, such as the traditional square alphabet blocks, LEGO® blocks, or even Jenga® pieces. (No blocks in the basement? Any small, three-dimensional, stackable objects will do).

After distributing blocks, say:

> **In a moment I'll ask you to take turns giving a building block to each person in your group of four. As you hand someone a block, tell that person about one gift, ability, or quality they have that contributes to making our group or our church a strong and holy "temple."**
>
> **Give the fourth block to yourself and tell the group what you think you can offer to build your church.**
>
> **After the first person has passed out all his or her blocks, use them to create a foundation for the structure you'll build with your remaining pieces—four at first, then adding four more at a time until you've used all 16 pieces to create a miniature building of some sort.**

Allow about five minutes for this affirmation activity, giving a one-minute warning before moving to the next section.

Note: *If time allows and your group as a whole isn't too large, ask the groups of four to combine their building with those of other small groups, creating one large structure.*

8. SPIRIT OF JESUS AFFIRMATION

(4 MINUTES REMAIN; USE 4 MINUTES IN THIS SECTION)

> Say: **We started our time together talking about belonging and group identity.**
>
> **The world is full of opportunities to belong—clubs, organizations, unions, hobby groups. Many even have symbols of belonging, such as logos, flags, stickers, even colors.**

The church sometimes uses symbols as signs of membership, too, but the underlying source of our unity, our identity, and our belonging is found elsewhere. An Old Testament prophet put his finger on it long ago.

Ask a volunteer to read aloud Joel 2:28-32a (pp. 929-930), and then ask another person to read aloud the "Reframing Jesus" sidebar on page 929.

Immediately after the second reader has finished, say:

The coming of the Spirit on all people as Joel envisioned happened for real after Jesus appeared to his followers soon after he was raised from the dead and ascended to God the Father.

The disciple Peter described that event this way...

Read aloud to the group Acts 2:16-24 (pp. 1138-1139), followed by the "Reframing Jesus" sidebar on page 1138. Then say:

It's the spirit of the risen Jesus that enlivens and sustains the church. And if you're a follower of Jesus, you're a part of all of it.

You belong. You're welcome here. You matter—to Jesus and his followers.

ABIDING IN JESUS

Being a part of the church includes interacting with other Christians, which can be one of the most challenging aspects of following Jesus. Consider your place in the community of Jesus by taking these steps:

A. Read these passages from the Bible:

- Psalm 133
- Colossians 3:12-17
- Ephesians 4:1-16
- Hebrews 10:23-25

❓ **What do you find attractive about Christian community as described in these passages? How do you sense the heart of Jesus behind these descriptions?**

❓ **Scan these passages again and count the number of times the word "love" appears. What's love got to do with Christian community?**

_____

_____

B. Reflect on this definition of community: Engaging with other disciples in common activities that sustain our life together and enlarge our capacity to experience more of God.

❓ **Where do you find Christian community? Or are you still searching?**

❓ **What are some "common activities" you think would be fun to explore in order to help you experience more of God?**

_____

_____

SESSION 7:
JESUS OF THE NEW CREATION

SESSION SUMMARY

In this session you'll discover Jesus' presence with us through eternity as the risen king and Savior, righteous judge, and the maker of a new creation. You'll also explore different ways we'll share in that new creation and enjoy eternal fellowship with Jesus.

ⓛ SUPPLIES NEEDED:

- A copy of the *Jesus-Centered Bible* for each person
- 3x5 cards or similar-sized slips of paper, 1 per person
- Pens, markers, or pencils
- A photocopy of the "Abiding in Jesus" take-home page for each person

---

1. GATHERING

(60 MINUTES REMAIN; USE 8 MINUTES IN THIS SECTION)

Warmly welcome participants, and then ask them to form small groups of four people.

> Say: **Congratulations! You've just gotten word that you've received a financial windfall. More like a *typhoon*-fall. And you're now wealthier than you've ever dreamed possible. Whether it was a surprise inheritance from Great-Aunt Edna or that lottery ticket you found in the parking lot that turned out to be a gargantuan winner—doesn't matter. What matters is that you are now insanely rich.**

To get to know the other zillionaires in your group of four, please share with them your answers to several questions.

❓ First, since you can now live anywhere, where will you make your home? For you, where is paradise on earth?

As for me, that would have to be...

Very briefly share where you'd live if you could live anywhere. Share where it is and why you'd pick that location.

Say: That's me...and you're all invited! In your small group, you now have two minutes to compare notes about where you consider to be paradise on earth.

Allow two minutes for groups to share. When 30 seconds remain, say: You have 30 seconds left to share. This lets groups know that if someone hasn't yet had shared, it's time to give that person a chance.

Say: Thanks. Here's a second question for you:

❓ What would you do with your time that you're not doing now?

Again, allow two minutes for sharing and give a 30-second warning.

Say: Thanks again. The last question is a double:

❓ Who would be with you there in paradise on earth—and how long could you live the life you've described?

Allow two minutes for sharing and give a 30-second warning.

2. THE NEW CREATION

(52 MINUTES REMAIN; USE 10 MINUTES IN THIS SECTION)

Say: **Thanks for sharing your ideas of what paradise might look like. And I'm assuming we're now all awaiting a call from Great-Aunt Edna's attorney.**

Maybe you noticed this in your group: We don't all have the same definition of "paradise." You might be a beach person and someone else in your group wants to live in the mountains.

But if you're a follower of Jesus, there's a paradise in your future—no need for Great-Aunt Edna. And today we're going to bring that paradise into focus. We'll look at what it is— and who we'll meet there.

Let's start by looking at some descriptions of two paradises.

Ask four volunteers to use their copies of the *Jesus-Centered Bible* to look up and be prepared to read aloud these four passages, in the order listed.

Reader 1: Genesis 1:1 (p. 5)

Reader 2: Genesis 2:8-15 (p. 6)

Reader 3: Revelation 21:1-2 (p. 1337)

Reader 4: Revelation 21:22–22:2 (pp. 1337-1338)

Ask the volunteers to read aloud their passages. When they've finished, say:

Two paradises: One in a garden as described in Genesis, and the other described as a "new heaven and new earth." In your group of four, talk about this:

❓ **What are the similarities and differences between the two paradises?**

Give everyone time to talk. When one minute of time remains, say: **Take another minute to wrap up your conversations, please.**

Draw attention back to yourself.

Say: **What did you discover as you talked in your group? What are the similarities and differences between these two paradises?**

Allow several responses.

3. PERSONAL PARADISE

(42 MINUTES REMAIN; USE 12 MINUTES IN THIS SECTION)

Thank participants for sharing their thoughts, both in small groups and in the whole group.

Say: **We missed joining Adam and Eve in the Garden of Eden, but there's still another paradise coming. In your group of four, talk about this:**

❓ **What aspect of the new creation as we heard it described in the Bible do you look forward to? Why?**

Allow up to four minutes for small groups to talk. Give a one-minute warning to wrap up conversation after three minutes have passed or when conversation is flagging in the small groups.

Say: **Thanks for sharing in your small group. Here's a second question for your small group to tackle, one that may sound...odd.**

You may remember when we were describing our personal paradises that we didn't all agree on the details—where we'd live, how we'd use our time, who would be there with us. One person's paradise is another person's not-so-much paradise.

So let me ask: What part of what's described as the coming new creation concerns you? Either it doesn't sound like paradise to you, or you have questions about it that aren't answered here, questions you wish you could ask.

In your small group, discuss this:

❓ **What concerns you about the new creation? Either it doesn't sound like paradise to you, or you have questions you wish you could ask.**

Allow up to four minutes for small groups to talk. Give a one-minute warning to wrap up conversation after three minutes have passed or when conversation is flagging in the small groups.

Say: **I'd love to know what concerns you might have. Is anyone willing to share with the whole group what came up in your small group?**

Allow several responses.

4. ADDITIONAL CLUES

(30 MINUTES REMAIN; USE 7 MINUTES IN THIS SECTION)

Say: **The prophet Isaiah envisioned the future coming of a new king and kingdom. Let's look at what Isaiah wrote to find clues that will help us know who'll be there in paradise.**

Ask a volunteer to read aloud Isaiah 11:1-10 (p. 711) as the others follow along in their *Jesus-Centered Bibles*. Then ask a volunteer to read aloud the Blue Explanation Box on page 711.

Ask the whole group to discuss the following questions. Allow several answers after each.

❷ **Which parts of Isaiah's vision do you think Jesus has fulfilled already?**

❷ **Which parts of Isaiah's vision do you think haven't yet come to pass?**

After discussing these two questions, ask participants to again huddle with their groups of four.

5. MAN-MADE PARADISE

(23 MINUTES REMAIN; USE 7 MINUTES IN THIS SECTION)

Say: **Some people are confident that some of what Isaiah described—a world of peace, harmony, and safety—can be achieved by people through communication and political compromise. They believe humankind can get to paradise without God's intervention.**

In your small group, talk about this:

❷ **How close can humans get to a paradise on earth apart from God? Why do you answer as you do?**

Allow up to four minutes for small groups to talk. Give a one-minute warning to wrap up conversation after three minutes have passed or when conversation is flagging in the small groups.

Say: **Is anyone willing to share with the whole group what came up in your small group? How close do you think humankind can get to paradise on earth apart from God— and why?**

Allow several responses.

6. WHO'S IN THE NEIGHBORHOOD?

(16 MINUTES REMAIN; USE 4 MINUTES IN THIS SECTION)

Thank participants for sharing their thoughts.

Say: **Our friend Isaiah was still a bit blurry on specifics concerning the coming new creation. Let's dig a bit deeper into several passages in the *Jesus-Centered Bible* to see what they can tell us.**

Ask participants to silently read Revelation 21:3-7 (p. 1337).

Say: **Notice that in verse 6 there are red letters—that's because this is a reference to Jesus. He's going to be in the new creation. We'll not only see him, but we'll be living in his neighborhood.**

Ask participants to silently read Revelation 22:3-5 (p. 1338).

Say: **Again we're told that we'll be with Jesus—the Lamb. No more worshipping him from a distance; we'll see him face to face.**

Ask the whole group:

❓ **How does it feel to know that you'll be in the literal presence of Jesus? And why do you answer as you do?**

7. THE NAMES OF JESUS

(12 MINUTES REMAIN; USE 5 MINUTES IN THIS SECTION)

Give a 3x5 card (or similar-sized slip of paper) to each person, along with a pen, pencil, or marker.

Say: **Revelation 22:4 says Jesus' followers will see his face and his name will be written on their foreheads. But which name?**

Take a moment and jot down which of Jesus' names you'd like to see. Maybe it's "Savior" because you deeply appreciate what he did for you on the cross. Maybe it's "Teacher" because his words have transformed your life. Maybe it's "friend."

Or maybe it's several words. Jot one or more of the names of Jesus that mean most to you on your card. Then, in your small group, share what's on your card and talk about this:

❷ Why did you pick the name or names you picked? Why are they so important to you, and what do they say about your relationship with Jesus?

Allow time for small groups to talk. Give a one-minute warning to wrap up conversation, and then draw attention back to yourself.

8. JUDGE JESUS

(7 MINUTES REMAIN; USE 3 MINUTES IN THIS SECTION)

Say to the group: **Hang onto those cards; you'll use them again.**

Some people see the new creation as anything but comforting. That's because they're aware of something that's coming along with the new creation.

Ask a volunteer to read aloud Daniel 7:9-10, 13-14 (p. 906). Then read aloud the Blue Explanation Box on page 906 while participants follow along in their *Jesus-Centered Bibles*.

Ask a volunteer to read aloud Revelation 1:13-18 (pp. 1321-1322), followed by the "Reframing Jesus" sidebar on page 1321.

Then say: **Small wonder this scene strikes fear into some people. The paradise waiting for us comes with a judgment. And Jesus is the judge.**

But notice that Jesus says for us to not be afraid. That's because Jesus' view of judgment isn't like our view. When Jesus judges, as he does in these passages, he's not condemning or punishing or extracting revenge. Instead, Jesus brings justice in the sense of making everything right again.

Righting wrongs and bringing new life to people can be done only by someone who has defeated death himself. And being in the presence of someone like that is cause for joy, not fear.

Let's celebrate that joy now.

9. JOY IN JESUS PRAYER

(4 MINUTES REMAIN; USE 3 MINUTES IN THIS SECTION)

Ask participants to stand in a circle or semi-circle. And ask them to hold the 3x5 cards they wrote on earlier.

Say: **There's still a lot we don't know about the new creation, but we do know this: Jesus is there...and as his followers we're invited to join him there.**

He will make all things new, and he will make all things right, and we can trust him and his grace and love.

With that in mind, let's celebrate the joy of what's coming for us—an eternal paradise with Jesus—by thanking him for who he is to us.

I'm going to open with prayer and then pause. When I pause, please call out the names you've written on your cards. That's who Jesus is to us—he's that and so much more. And it's okay if we sometimes talk at the same time; he's very able to hear all of us at the same time!

Jesus, we're in awe of you and what you've done for us. You gave your life so we could be in relationship with you, and your love and mercy have never faltered. Thank you for walking with us, for forgiving us, for inviting us into your forever family.

Thank you, Jesus, for being our...

Pause to allow time for participants to speak aloud the words they wrote on their cards. When they're finished, close your prayer by saying...

Jesus, we're yours. And we love you.

Amen.

10. CONCLUSION

(1 MINUTE REMAINS; USE 1 MINUTE IN THIS SECTION)

Say: **Thank you for being part of our journey through the big themes of the Bible. I pray that you've encountered Jesus in some new and rewarding ways. I'd like to close our time together by reading you these words from the New Testament book of Jude:**

"Now all glory to God, who is able to keep you from falling away and will bring you with great joy into his glorious presence without a single fault. All glory to him who alone is God, our Savior through Jesus Christ our Lord. All glory, majesty, power, and authority are his before all time, and in the present, and beyond all time! Amen." (Jude 24-25)

ABIDING IN JESUS

There are numerous theories and speculations about what happens at the end of time. One of the best ways to keep our eyes and hearts on Jesus in the midst of all these ideas is to simply read the Scriptures. Try playing around with this idea:

• Each day for a week, reread Revelation 21 and 22 from your *Jesus-Centered Bible.*

• On Tuesday, read the "Reframing Jesus" sidebar on page 1337.

• On Thursday reflect on the Jesus Question on page 1338.

• Write your thoughts down in a journal or some other form of permanent record.

• Share your notes and thoughts with a trusted friend or spiritual mentor.

_____

_____

_____

_____

_____

_____

_____

_____

_____

_____

Center on Jesus With These Additional Jesus-Centered Resources

JESUS-CENTERED BIBLE

Throughout the Old Testament, blue letters point out remarkable connections to Jesus, pulling you into the bigger story. And the New Testament includes a variety of thought-provoking questions that prompt you to reframe your understanding of Jesus (and yourself).

Available in hardcover and a variety of colors in imitation leather.

OTHER JESUS-CENTERED RESOURCES

- **Journals** in a variety of colors—perfect for recording new insights into Jesus.
- **Devotionals**—daily readings and activities for anyone who wants to draw closer to Jesus.
- **Coloring books**—tap into your creative side as you tap into Jesus.

To learn more about living a Jesus-centered life, visit JesusCenteredLife.com or your favorite Christian bookseller.